An Author's View on Book Marketing

Sherrie Lynn

DISCLAIMER

Copyright © 2018 by Sherrie Lynn
All rights reserved.

No part of this book may be reproduced, scanned, or distributed in any manner whatsoever without written permission from the author except in the case of brief quotation embodied in critical articles and reviews.

Table Of Contents

INTRODUCTION

In 2017 I challenged myself to write four books in one year. Although I consider the romance suspense, *'In Too Deep'* finished, I know it can be better, so depending on how you look at it, I accomplished my goal after releasing *'Every Blue Moon'* and the novella, *'Work Ethic'* from the Modern Romance Suspense series earlier this year. I will make no such promise in 2018. An author's view always starts off being a good idea until there is either too much or too little information on the chosen subject. In this case there is no end to the information on book marketing. This view includes paperback books as well as eBooks. I talk about my own personal experiences as an author and what fellow authors have expressed along their book marketing journey plus the basics of what we should do to get the word out about our new book. Every author's experiences bring something different to your marketing efforts.

CHAPTER 1

WHEN DO I START?

While this may sound a bit ridiculous, the most essential and important steps to take toward promoting a published book can begin long before the actual writing of the book. Even a few years before the book is published, building a network of supporters and reviewers can be started. Keep track of everyone you met as researching and writing the book commences. Special attention should be paid to those who demonstrate a genuine enthusiasm for the author and the project. As the project starts and comes into the limelight; keep in touch with these people. An occasional email can be sent to them, or keep in touch via social networking sites such as LinkedIn or Facebook. If the author of the book wants to make large sales, the author must make sure the book is of high quality regarding the contents, the material and free from grammatical blunders and plagiarism. Make sure your content is unique.

Marketing is defined as the promotion, distribution, and selling of a product or service; which includes market research and advertising. The typical goal of marketing is to generate interest of the buyers in the product and create leads or prospects. The activities involved in marketing includes consumer research which is designed to identify the needs of the customers, product development which means designing innovative products to meet existing or hidden needs, advertising the products to raise awareness and build the brand, and pricing products and services to maximize long-term revenue.

Revenue maximization is a function of how many sales are made within a period of time. Therefore, making good sales of the published book is of paramount importance. Sales activities in book publishing are focused on converting prospects to actual paying readers. Sales occasionally might involve directly interacting with the prospects to persuade them to purchase the book. Not all authors' desire to market their books this way and prefer remaining at their computer working on the next book. Their marketing will consist mainly of outsourcing by way of promotion companies. No form of marketing can guarantee sales, but if you do nothing, readers have no idea your book is now available to order.

CHAPTER 2

WRITE SOMETHING GOOD

This sounds obvious, but there are countless numbers of badly-written, poorly-edited self-published books all over the world. Because there are a lot of tools out there that are so easy to use, there is a temptation to get anything out there, without going through the rigors of research, proofreading by a professional and editing, in hopes of quick discovery and viral success. If the book is to make a good sale, the author should not give in to that temptation. The quality of the contents of the book has much to do with creating readers' interest which facilitates more requests for the book.

All books should be read by a beta reader before the editing process to get their opinion of your book, especially with fiction. Many authors skip this part by not having access to avid readers who are knowledgeable enough to trust their opinion. Plus, this adds to the production cost if you must pay them. Also, some beta readers may take too long to get back to you as we have our own timetable on how long it should take to do anything. I'm more concerned with allowing too many people to gain access to my work before it is published but it helps to have people you trust to read your manuscript and provide valuable feedback that can potentially make the book better. Don't be sceptical but proud if one says, don't change a thing. It's perfect just the way it is.

Once you've made any changes based on your beta readers' opinions and suggestions, the service of a competent copy and grammar editor can be hired to do the proofreading and editing job. Remember a copy editor and a grammar editor is looking at two different things when reading your manuscript and important to have both. Authors should know that marketing is essential, but all the marketing in the world would not help a product that is not of decent quality.

No matter how you acquire your editor, Upwork, Fiverr, low-cost freelance websites or anyone claiming to be the best editor in the world whose fee will reflect this statement, always proofread what you get back from your editor. Their editing style or process can make changes you don't agree with. For this reason, I always and have always had to make necessary corrections and address suggestions from the first editor before sending it off to a completely different editor. This returned copy should have fewer corrections or changes, but you must proofread it again before sending it to your formatter. Some editors tend to think highly of themselves and can do no wrong. But recently; one wrote "a box" instead of "a book." Don't assume they don't make mistakes.

When you get your manuscript back from your formatter, you must proofread it again before uploading for publication. Make sure you hire a formatter who know the requirements for the eBook or paperback publishing service you're going to use. Make sure you get the correct file type that will upload with no problems.   KDP, Lulu or Smash words just to name a few. E-book formatting is entirely different from paperback formatting. Some big-name authors I noticed did not bother to format their eBook professionally, and it looks terrible. For some reason that bothers me, I want to see a neatly formatted page when reading my eBook and everything that can be enabled.

Another important thing that will help sell a book beyond the quality of the work itself is reviews. This should be done by a reputable author of a well-known reputation. Also, the foreword of the book should be written by a well-known scholar whose experience and wealth of knowledge is appreciated by a larger audience. The book will also gain quite a bit of credibility in readers' minds when they see more than a handful of thoughtful reviews. Writing a 'Forward' for other authors is also a way to network and promote yourself and your books. While mostly done in non-fiction books; being asked to write a Forward or Preface is a compliment and a win; win for everyone involved.

CHAPTER 3

CULTIVATE A *POSITIVE ATTITUDE* ABOUT BOOK PROMOTION

It is in your best interest to do so. Book promotion is like a story-telling, the story to be told is why the book is written, how it can help others, and how the world will benefit from the book. All these should be explicitly stated in the promotion.

If a positive attitude can be developed about book promotion, people will pick up on it, and tune in immediately. Some writers do not want to partake in marketing/promoting their work, they believe marketing is the publisher's job and promoting their own book should not be their responsibility. Indie authors don't have the luxury of thinking like this. If they don't market the book, no one else will.

A little bit of investment can go a long way here. There are all kinds of ways to use paid promotion to spread the word about the already published book. Email promotions can be run through book promotion sites that list discount deals, and send out daily emails to their respective subscribers. While there are so many to choose from, here are a few of the most popular that cost little or nothing to register your book. These websites include Fussy Librarian; who allow subscribers also to indicate their taste in tone like you only read mysteries without profanity, violence, and sex. Bargain Booksy; favour free and bargain books like Ereader News Today. Keep in mind that many of these websites only want books priced under $1.99, and their primary objective is to get you to sign up your book under their terms which may conflict with your overall objective. But don't discount the potential benefits of adjusting to their requirements. Other websites can find you, by providing your business email address on your website just under your name. They are in the business to make money, so you have no problem reaching out to authors looking to promote their books. Study each website to be clear on how they go about promoting books; especially *where* they promote so your type of book reaches the desired target audience.

About Emails: When I first started writing and promoting my books, I felt my email box was being flooded with junk mail. I recently got around to deleting over three thousand emails from the inbox alone. But I checked each one, moving good ones to the business file to study later. Of course, a lot of it is junk mail meaning something you have no interest in. For example, enhancement or pornography is moved to the spam folder. Yes, you can create folders to help organize your emails. The same deleting process should take place in your spam folder as some of your emails arrive there and never make it to your inbox. Companies you're working with will advise you to check your spam folder for the email they just sent to verify your email address. Mark that email as not spam for future emails to land in your inbox.

Your trash folder is just that trash. Occasionally, I have deleted an important email by mistake and found it in the trash. As a result, I set my trash folder or trash bin to empty every thirty days whereas prior to this, it was like my inbox with over three thousand unread emails. No, I don't need furniture right now or a walk-in bathtub, maybe later; because you are a published author, it is assumed that you have more money than you know what to do with. A time may come when you can purchase whatever you want and buy great gifts for friends and family. This is the motivation for such random emails looking to be the first to sell you their product. But wait until you are on solid ground financially.

CHAPTER 4

YOUR MEDIA KIT

According to Wikipedia, a press kit often referred to as a media kit; is a pre-packaged set of promotional materials of a person, company, or organization distributed to members of the media for promotional use. They are often distributed to announce a release or for a news conference. A basic for book marketing is professionally printed business cards with the book cover on one side and the author's contact information on the other side. Include the books ISBN so it can be put in the database and be accessible to most of the book distributors.   While most publishing services allegedly take care of all this for you, there is still the original way to publish your book through book printers which the cost is high, but you get to control pricing better. You can still sell your books directly from your website and mail them out yourself or sign up on Amazon as a seller. Other sellers will eventually obtain your book. I can only strongly advise you not to be a book pirate depriving authors of their royalties after all their hard work.

A few words biography: The purpose of the author biography is to tell the reader the qualities possessed, the wealth of experience, and the qualifications that uniquely qualified the writer to have written that book. For example, this book is not a technical, textbook but an author's view. I'm conscious of not making it difficult to understand as that was the point to help authors who are just starting out or who never bothered to read any book on book marketing. The more books you read on book marketing, you will discover just how technical it can be, especially for the writer who just want to write. I find that I need to focus on non-fiction after a year of writing a fiction story. Much like the real world, I need to detach from issue driven characters and all their drama that come before the happy ending.

A 'one-sheet' for the book: a one-page description of the book should be written on the other side, and this must include a few positive short blurbs or excerpts from the book plus review quotes from your beta readers, professional colleagues and friends in the description. Some say a book blog is necessary, in which the updates and corrections respond to reader comments and suggestions. This book blog may become the basis for the second edition of the book that will include an address; such remarks are from various sources. However, media kits have changed quite a bit since I first started writing over thirty years ago. Kits were designed for snail mail book distributors and book review publications with a suggested minimum mailing of 500 that also includes a free copy of your book.

The new online distribution method is less expensive. Do your homework and find out how each book review publication accepts press kits. Such publications are distributed to professional book buyers around the world who will decide what books will make it into real offline bookstores and chain stores that have a book section. Make sure the publication is geared toward your type of book. Review Publications that surprised me were military for military base stores, history and war publications. I was thinking; who would be interested in the details of every war ever fought? Of course, I eventually came across a real person who was obsessed with this type of information and already owned a library of such books. The latest information surface over the years; so more books are written on the subject. Of course, my faith-based books can fall into various publications but believe it or not; some Christian review publications still don't believe in Christian fiction because the bookstores don't encourage or believe in Christian fiction. But this only opens the door to a niche market and a chance to have your own Christian fiction bookstore and or review publication. Since my faith-based characters are multi-cultural leaning toward contemporary African American stories, this saves me money and narrow my choices for review publications.

Allegedly, Amazon reviews are amazingly effective. Everyone from book buyers to publishers reads them. While many books on marketing put a lot of emphasis on book reviews from publications and individual book readers and those who write book reviews for a living, I'm exhausted from chasing after book reviews mainly because, based on one person's opinion, it's a good chance you might get a negative review that can hurt your book sales. While bad reviews have been known to generate sales out of peaked interest, there are those who base their book buying solely on complimentary reviews. For the sake of generating sales, try to get three to five good to decent reviews posted on your book before any harsh ones. If you can, remind the reviewer not to give away the contents.

My best suggestion from an author's view is to type 'press kit' in the search engine of your choice. From there, click on images to see the many ways in which a media kit can be designed. This way if it's ten, twenty years from now when you finally finish your next book, you can see the most up to date information. The above info reminds you of what should be included. With my first book, I came up with the idea to get everything on one page, making use of both sides in a brochure style. People have short attention spans and want everything up front to save time. Professional marketing firms or large publishing houses might disagree with this, but they can afford to create a colourful, two-sided, four-page press kit. If you're operating strictly online, now you can too. Being creative with your press kit is an effective way to make you and your book stand out from the rest. Remember; just because you send out four beautiful pages of your media kit do not guarantee those pages will get read. More importantly, keep in mind that reviewers write your book review based on what is in your media kit so don't short change your book description. Don't exaggerate but make sure it sizzles and pop with enthusiasm.

CHAPTER 5

BUILD A NICE "PLATFORM" AND EXPOSURE

A platform is defined as whatever plan and methods an author uses to connect with readers and sell books. This can be achieved by using online means such as website, social media, Amazon author pages, and an email list.

Website: A website is needed to spread the word and keep the conversation going. It is a place for fans to contact the author and a way to build an email list. Contents can be created on websites like wix.com or type free websites in the search engine. If you're clueless about setting this up, fiverr.com offers setup for a fee. Though, much traffic may not be pulled at the beginning, after a while (be patient!), if there are engaging contents and good keywords, there will be clicks, and the email signups start to come in. Some authors keep the conversation going in other areas such as their blog, video blog or mainly Facebook fan page.

Email list: This is a serious battle, but worth the fight. As a new author, getting people interested enough to take the ride through emails is tough. Mail Chimp or Constant Contact could be used to manage the email list and campaigns because it is an excellent tool at an affordable price. This is something that is often encouraged, but if you know you're not ready to do anything with that email list, especially when you only have one book and nothing else to offer, this can be something beneficial after publishing two to twelve books or started a promotion company of your own.

Social media: Social media and how to work it, covers so much territory it deserves its own book. But briefly, Facebook, Twitter, and YouTube are just some of the social media websites that are very helpful in doing book promotion online, but this process should not be overdone. Care should be taken in choosing the right medium for your book, for example, if creating a graphic novel — very visual is the choice; Facebook and Pinterest would be the best choice. Journalist writing non-fiction, Twitter will be appropriate, so choose the one that best fits your type of book.

Publishing service author and book pages: If an author self-publishes when uploading your file for publication, every space provided should be used if relevant to your current project. Make sure you did not check off box's that can hurt your book sells. Every service is different and normally provides a detailed explanation or form to answer all your questions. A good example is to ask yourself if you want your book available through Kindle Unlimited upon initial release. Once a book is old, I don't have a problem with that but a new release, for me, no way. In the book description, make it strong and compelling to grab reader attention. Your product description is your sales letter. Make it good.

I hired a freelance writer to write my book description, and it was horrible and unusable. I studied many other book descriptions and came up with an award-winning one of my own. Throughout this process I'm constantly saying to myself, 'hey wait, you're a writer, you can write your own press release, your own sales letter or article and will save time and money.

KEYWORDS

Remember to list good keywords while uploading your book. Most publishing services offer an author page where you can link to your latest blog posts and tweets. As a writer, you will have days when you want to comment on current events in your life and about world news. This is what your blog is for as well as gathering fans that can translate into book sales. Make your blog somehow; tie into the books your offering. After a while, as your blog entries gain interests, the reader is excited to see you have books available to order.

CHAPTER 6

WRITE VARIOUS ARTICLES ON THE BOOK

Every field has e-zines, websites, and newsletters that advocate or deal with the subject of your book. Search for these, once they are found, look through them and figure out which ones talk to the audience about the book. Contact those sites or publications and pitch articles that will be of interest to their readers. Schedule articles to appear around the time the book will appear in bookstores and on Amazon. For example, if the book will be on sale in the bookstores and on Amazon in mid-June, schedule the articles to appear in July, August, and September.

Remember to pitch articles early, because many magazines and e-zines have a 3-6-month lead time. Make sure the book title is mentioned somewhere in the article. In online articles, link the book title to its order page so readers can click over and buy the book. You can write your own articles or work with freelance writers on Upwork or Fiverr. Whatever website you go with, choose your article writer wisely. Make sure you provide them with the most valuable information you want in your article.

I would suggest you write the best third person article you can within the word count you want and give that to your freelance writer as a guideline. They might request a word file or pdf version of the book to work their magic. Try to limit doing this as it is how other sellers get your book. If what you get back is an unusable piece of crap, you can try to get your money back, request a revision or just move on to another article writer. If you're not wowed by it, your reader will not be either. You should be excitedly thinking, 'is this my book?' And tempted to order it yourself.

In my experiences, I've always had to make some changes and whip it into shape before submitting, but the hired freelancer provides their sales letter expertise giving me something to work with. As the author, you know your book better than anyone and should make sure all your articles represent the book your reader is about to purchase.

Get Mentioned in email Blasts: Look for organizations in the same field as your book that send large-volume emails. Try to get the book reviewed in their email or newsletter.

When the number of people receiving the emails is several thousand or more, it is sometimes referred to as an email blast.

Speak at Conferences: As a published author, you have the qualifications necessary to speak at conferences. Contact conference organizers some months in advance. At first, registration may be required and pay a fee to speak, later, when awareness has been created, and you or your book is well known, conferences may seek you out for another presentation, and may even be paid to speak. If you have a fear of public speaking, I suggest joining toastmasters.org. This is what was suggested to me by an audience member after shaking like a leaf during my first reading. There is a materials fee to join but serious about getting you in front of other members to speak at every single meeting. You can shop around visiting until you find the meeting location you prefer. Find one that goes by the book creating a professional environment. While stage fright can return being away from the podium for a while, I enjoyed being part of this. Toastmasters International is an organization where you can move up the ranks to the point of paying gigs and hosting your own meetings. The last time I had a reading; I was hogging the mic and even had the audience laughing.

The book can be officially launched: For significant milestones- the completion of the manuscript, editors and beta readers you know personally, and finally the arrival of the finished books. Key people involved in pulling your book together especially any reporters or political figures you know can be brought together for a party or book launching. At the rented hall/house party/book launching, short excerpts from the book could be read and answer questions about the project. I have such a grand vision of my book launch; I just couldn't settle for something small scale so in the past chose to skip this part of the book marketing process. Today, this is something that can be done online with a big marketing push just before launch day.

Most writers are naturally reclusive and would rather be sitting at their computer working on the next book. The mere thought of attending a party with real people and not characters of their own making can bring on a serious anxiety attack. I suggest no one put together a surprise launch as the author is likely not to show up or will disappear soon after arriving. Hosting a launch or promotional party online, the author is not required to be there. Just make sure the press kits and books are available.

Give a good packaging and positioning: The book packaging must be attractive of excellent quality and lavish with all forms of aesthetic design to attract the prospective buyers.   Different ideas might seem overwhelming, but remember, one thing at a time needs to be done. You will soon be reaching your audience. Slower than you want, but faster than you think, you may become a best-selling author.

CHAPTER 7

NETWORKING

Networking is also an area that can be another whole book for there are so many moving parts involved but briefly; Family and friends would be at the top of your networking efforts. For those interested in helping you market your book. But strangely, many authors have announced they are on their own when it comes to family and friends. Pride may play a role in this as men and women are reluctant to admit they can't read or spell very well and don't see themselves asking all the questions they need to be answered to help you promote your book. Our ego can stop us from helping someone we always felt was beneath us and can't see themselves in such a subservient position to this person. But don't forget to show your appreciation to those friends and family members that do visibly support and help in your marketing efforts. Posting and sharing are free and not rocket science.

Authors helping authors is next on your networking list. If you come across a book you really like, feel free to tell everyone you know about it. I'm currently reading on Kindle,

'*How I Sold 80,000 Books* 'by Alinka Rutkowska. This book came across my Facebook newsfeed with the eBook being offered for free. I actually started not to download it but, what did I have to lose? This book is now on my recommended reading list for authors looking to market their books. My research involves what is already being said so that I can focus on other neglected areas of book marketing. I've already implemented some of her suggestions and only halfway through. The paperback edition is now on Amazon for $13.99. Whenever I read where it suggested offering a free book, I'm like, no way, the point is to make money. But here is an example of book promotion with authors helping authors; with a free book.

Networking covers a lot of little-known territories. You can investigate genre websites, and reach out as much as possible to offer guest postings, interviews, book reviews, or whatever is deemed fit that site might find interesting, or live readings at physical locations like public libraries. Readers love purchasing books from the author and better yet ask questions on how to get started in this business. Make sure you have flyers or bookmarks to hand out at your readings. Be creative but get them to your purchase page.

Join A Networking Group or Forum: Every field of study has at least one or two environments that people of common interest do relate and share experience and findings. When I first started out, Yahoo groups were super popular and perhaps still are. In my opinion, one of the best informative networking sites I've come across so far; start with Midwest Book Review. A serious author/publisher who wants to make good sales should find a means of joining these forums to create awareness of his/her new publication. An author can contribute to them (the groups) freely, give professional advice and by so doing, the intention of being well known will be achieved which will translate to more sales of the book. I was doing this initially to gain additional information surrounding writing and publishing but surprised at just how much I could contribute based on my own experiences. I didn't see it as promoting myself or my books but ultimately fascinated with the different things other authors were doing, like creating online magazines and newsletters, publishing new author's and offering predesigned book covers.

CHAPTER 8

HOW DO I GENERATE BOOK SALES?

When looking to generate book sales, an author must see their books from the reader's point of view. As a reader yourself, consider how you find the books you want and with modern technology, in what way would you prefer to read it? For some, writing a book is easy and interesting. Book writing is a career to some people while other writers do it as a hobby. Career or as a hobby, the beauty of writing is getting it to readers. The level of readership counts in motivating an author which may translate into being well known and making some sales on the next books published. The hard part of writing a book is neither getting it published nor the actual writing itself but to get it to the targeted audience.

An author is elated if his/her book gets to the targeted audience and beyond, but while there is a craze for some to offer free books, not all books can be free because of production cost. This is especially true for paperbacks depending on how you choose to produce your paperback or hardcover copies. I've heard readers say they skip over free online books and have no interest in reading one assuming it must be something wrong with it if it is free.   You have the option to say, 'for a limited time only.' In the process of marketing your book, there will be instances where signing away free copies can benefit you in the future.

Some readers like me prefer holding an actual book in hand and while the reader has your book already downloaded, may still decide to purchase a hardcover copy. This means making more sales on just one book. In the case of self-help books, readers might also prefer it in audiobook form to listen to in their car during morning rush hour commute. Also, several authors in the same genre have published numerous topics and copies of books. Then, to stand out among equals and to become outstanding in this business means offering your book in every format available. Today, your book can go way beyond being displayed on the shelf in a bookstore.

There are some things to be put in place as a potential entrepreneur will do. No matter what type of book written, or plan to write, there are many ways to reach the targeted audience. Each of the means listed costs little or nothing in implementation, and each of them works in its own way. One or more may be perfect for the individual author.

CHAPTER 9

POST & MAKE ONLINE VIDEOS

This is an area I love. Today and only recently, product marketing on social media has taken it to a whole new level and made it easier to post an exciting video promoting your book or product. How many times have you heard someone say, 'I'm sure it's a YouTube video on that subject.' And if not, this is your opportunity to create one or certainly a better one. Five minutes or a series of videos with the author talking about key issues in the book can be made and put on social media. The book title and universal resource locator (URL) should then be put at the bottom of the video screen and in the credits. Your kids or young people around you are often more knowledgeable of this; then you might think and would love to know they played a part in your success as an author, not to mention encouraging a business mind for their own future. Author Jenna Moreci has created one of the most exciting video blogs where her style is apparent, funny and most of all informative which bring in new subscribers all the time. The result is awareness of her book and generating book sales. Due to site changes, I currently have three different channels that showcase whatever videos I have including music artists I did promotional concert edits for. I do plan to come up with a tutorial series eventually that will focus more on books. When you can start off organizing your marketing plan from the beginning, maintaining the same theme, you are more likely to generate sales of your product. Various products mean finding a way to bring it altogether avoiding any confusion. In my case, music videos of real artists lead to my novel, Backstage Pass, The Jade Sheldon Story which is inspired by actual events.

Book video trailers can be put on several of the many video-sharing websites. I normally work with websites such as fiverr.com where one gig can submit your promotion video to sixty or more video sites like YouTube. I was surprised to discover just how many video sharing sites there are around the world. But some video sharing sites are too themed, focused in one area and may not be an appropriate choice for marketing books or the type of book you have. When I outsource by submitting to the over sixty different video sharing websites, it is my way of mass marketing; mainly with non-fiction books. Most people are looking for personal growth or learning something new. Non-fiction is said to generate more sales worldwide. Why do I say this? Because it is reiterated in most books on marketing plus, when I meet people from another country, I ask them.

Your website address should be placed in the back of all your books. If your reader purchased your non-fiction, they would check your website or webpage to see what other exciting books you have to offer. If they happen to enjoy fiction as well, your books can be purchased directly from your website. Make sure the books on your website is linked to the ordering page.

Many of us already know how to upload a video to YouTube; the beauty of this is, the video can be embedded on the author's website and other social media websites if that feature is offered. Working with websites like fiverr.com is an affordable gamble that may or may not pay off. Any form of paid marketing, no matter the size of the firm or outrageous fee works the same way. Sales are not guaranteed. Set your budget in advance or start off by doing it all yourself to save money. This will require trial &era, time and research.

CHAPTER 10

SOCIAL MEDIA

If you are the author of a newly written book or the person in charge of increasing its sales, book marketing can be a fun challenge. Online self-publishing platforms have encouraged many people to write and publish books by themselves on a variety of subjects, and the internet public is spoiled with the numerous choices. I've had mixed feelings about offering a free book but after reading a Facebook comment on how this disabled veracious reader couldn't get to bookstores or the public library, or afford many books, truly appreciated the free books available online. With my Kindle, I have downloaded books from the public library. When they are due back, it will no longer be on your Kindle. While most authors are looking to make money from their writing, there are those who feel getting the content to as many readers as possible is even more important. This only means you will have to be creative in other ways to generate income. But the Internet is a great platform to empower your book marketing campaign and help you reach people who might never have heard of your book otherwise.

Marketing creates awareness of your offering and getting people to the front door of your sales process. The sales process, not the marketing process is what puts money in your bank account. Do not invest in marketing with no effective sales process in place!

Ask yourself if you have a solid sales framework in place:

What is your sales conduit? Do you have a system in place so that once someone expresses an interest in what you are offering, there is a process in place to close the deal?

Do you believe in what you are offering? Keep in mind; this is social media, not an advertisement. You are making new acquaintances and friends. If you want to be successful, you should care if what you are offering will be valuable and useful.

Have you considered the various ways to connect what you're offering in conversation? You should have dozens, hundreds, even thousands of ideas which can lead to *talking about your book.* Why? Conversations are two-way interactions, and your potential buyer needs to lead the conversation as much as you do. It is much easier to talk about the subject matter that they led the conversation to, than someplace your trying to force it to go. We all like to talk about something more when it was our idea to talk about it.

You might be surprised at how few people can answer any of those questions. Every person who is successfully making money using social media as their major or only avenue of marketing knows the answers. So, answer them as best you can. If any of the answers are answered in vague, uncertain terms, then you do not know the answer. If you do not know the answer to any of those questions, you are going to have a tough time earning any money using the social media arena. If your social interaction skills need a boost, your budget will have to factor in hiring an administrator for your fan pages.

I'm guilty of not always providing a link to the purchase page when posting flyers of the book cover on social media. Book reviews and excerpts along with the flyer or book cover always generate more interest. The business size or postcard size flyer will say, 'Order on Amazon' or available at most online & better bookstores. Ok, say the reader is interested but will have to open another browser, type in Amazon, once here, type in your author name and the title of the book if they still remember all this. If not; click back to Facebook, Instagram, wherever they came across your post, to get the correct information. Well, you get the idea. Consider all the distracting side ads and popups, including messenger that can snatch the reader's attention.

If I'm really interested in this book, I will do all of this. I may want more information before deciding, and this is where your preview and product description lock in the sale. Providing a direct route to the purchase page will likely generate more sales. I have mixed feelings about landing pages as I feel this give the reader too much time to change their mind. I will consider it a part-two of the overall marketing plan. Landing pages are normally designed like an exciting sales letter that should jump out visually and briefly contain the best of your press kit and your best article. Make the words large and easy to read. A lot of tiny writing can make people say forget it; I'm not reading all of this. Don't forget the link to the purchase page. Make it clearly visible.

CHAPTER 11

WORK YOUR ONE YEAR PLAN

Don't think about a published book as competing for precious reader-hours. More books, fewer sales may be because of the publishers spending nothing or little on marketing to try to reach those increasingly rare readers. Less help from the publisher or yourself means that the author, you must do more to get the word out.

It's worth noting, however, if Marketing becomes a sales support function focused only on the now, the future can become lost. Again, plan on following the promotion plan--perhaps an hour a day—and let it run for at least a year. Resolve in doing something every day on promotion, if you can put together a promotion team, go for it. Your team consists of people who sincerely want to help market and promote your book sales. Provide them with the information they need to do so. The author must still use discretion with any help that is offered.

Without Marketing, Sales Suffers!

A remarkable book will generate word-of-mouth publicity. If one person reads it; finds it interesting and amazing, that person may recommend it to his or her friends. They will recommend it to their friends, and by doing so, the book gets across to the largest audience ever. This is the best publicity that can be gotten. Keep in mind this can happen within a three to the five-year radius. Books have an incubation period with the minimum being three years before recognition or generating real sales. Remember eighteen-year-olds become adults every four years which mean a new generation of adults who are just discovering your book. When writing, keep this in mind. My writing teacher told me always to think ten years beyond any current project.

There should be a reasonable price placed on the book. Market survey of similar books should be done before fixing a price. The price should not be too small in order not to lower its standard and should not be too high not to discourage prospective buyers. So, the price must be reasonable, competitive and affordable. Remember to participate in book exhibitions like the annual book expo America. Check search results for a list of popular, yearly book events. My favourite is on cruise ships with a notable jazz quartet.

CHAPTER 12

BOOK MARKETING IN TODAY'S WORLD

Today, many believe marketing your books online will be a game-changer for authors and indie publishers. If you've been paying attention to what's going on in the publishing industry right now, then you'll know that eBook sales are skyrocketing while paperback and physical book sales are declining. The future is eBooks, especially for independent authors who don't have distribution through the big book retailers like Barnes &Noble, Target, Wal-Mart, etc. But the ability to acquire that is becoming more popular as entrepreneurs are looking to fill any niche that is potentially profitable. Feel free to post website links for book marketing on my Facebook fan page. Follow me on Facebook. Like and Share.

For writers with paperback books, it's worth considering selling your idle books for cash. List your unwanted books on eBay. The prices you can ask for most books are meager unless you have a collector's edition of a book. While the reader is ecstatic, one of the biggest pains with selling your used and unwanted books on Amazon is the small sum you are offered. When selecting an online book buyback service, it pays to stick with a merchant who is a member of the Better Business Bureau just for peace of mind and hopefully quality service.

Book marketing in today's world is about technology and encouraged to use it for the greater good of all humanity. While we individually can write something, and put it out there, whatever genre, be conscious of what you put into the reading world. It is tempting to rush this process with the vision of that pot of gold at the end of the rainbow. I'm tempted to buy Bitcoins right now. It's a gamble just like writing a book. Some of us come by it naturally while other's struggle. Keep in mind; a good book is a matter of opinion. Although it is your best asset, making book sales has nothing to do with if you're a good writer. It's about being good at marketing your book. Write the best book you can write. Be innovative. Your book can grow legs.

SUMMARY

When you finally do start making money with your books, think ahead, think about the long run. Royalties are to my understanding not considered a real income because they are too inconsistent. I'm thinking author's pay cash for big ticket items like a condo, home or car and importantly invest in something that will generate another income; a franchise, commercial property or stocks if you're knowledgeable in these areas. Authors need guaranteed income to maintain everyday needs. Assessments on a condo; yearly taxes on a home not to mention monthly utility and food bills.

Keep writing and releasing books as each book have a selling period that will eventually come to a slow crawl if not a complete halt. Marketing and promoting in our world today mean you must do your homework as new avenues are opening all the time. While researching how to market your books, consider not every website or suggestions is right for your type of book or will fit your budget. One author picked one marketing source and no other and claim to have sold many books. Another author consistently went at every single suggestion that came across her desk and now doing very well with her books. Each year revamp your marketing strategies. Consistency is my friend and yours as well.

Another good point is, be leery of people who do something for nothing. Be clear on what compensation is expected for their generosity. Once you're on the New York Times bestsellers list and Tyler Perry turns your book into a movie, they will rematerialize with their attorney and their hand out saying, 'remember what I did for you.'   Being too generous can leave you broke no matter how many books you've written and had published. Remember, a well-written review can boost your own book sales, so don't forget to post your positive review of this book on the purchase page. It would be greatly appreciated. This is just the beginning.

MORE BOOKS BY S. LYNN

Novel

A Forward Motion

Set in the seventies this is a coming-of-age interracial love story about a group of friends trying to negotiate a course between the straight life of education and church-going and the wild side of drugs, nightclubs and sex. The characters innocent but often-gritty performance makes this a multi-cultural eclectic thrill ride! Future history will determine if we're all just standing still, traveling in circles or moving in a Forward Motion.

"Crystal?" He laughed. "Crystal Alexander."

She smiled stifling a blush as the memory of their intimacy flashed into full view as if it was just yesterday.

He shoved his fingers in the top of his jeans as another guy walked up beside him frowning at her. "You remember my cousin Nash."

Crystal just nodded at him never having had much to say to Nash in the past.

"You two would cross paths." He said non-too flatteringly.

Crystal was preoccupied with Julian's masculinity oozing from his thicker sexy physic. He appeared much taller than she remembered him to be.

"So, what's going on with you these days?" Julian asked.

"I was just about to put an investigative journalist onto the ill practices of this mall. I have a B.A. in public relations and going for my master's in political science. Yet, I'm still followed around like some type of criminal."

"Well don't let us stop progress." Nash commented. "Come on man." He addressed Julian.

"You're a political activist. Why am I not surprised?" Julian said with an amused smirk.

"They'll squash you like a bug." Nash threw in sarcastically laughing.

She threw Nash a knowing look. "I ran into your friend Raul a couple years ago in Florida. Did you guys actually attend classes or just a crash course on sexually transmitted deceases?"

"Ouch!" Julian cringed.

NOVEL

Backstage Pass!

The Jade Sheldon Story

"He's had a lot of girlfriends." She eagerly supplied. "Never the same one for long. I ought to know."

I glanced at her with a confident knowing smile but remained silent refusing to play this game. On the ride home, I wanted to interrogate Reed. Stars words had bothered me more than the old wedding photos, jolting me out of that ridiculous happily ever after dream I kept falling into.

Reed had more than one appeal. I was used to him and hated the idea of having to start all over with a new guy. Money wasn't everything, especially when you have it, but not only was Reed among the prominent of society; he also came from a two parent, spiritually grounded family background like myself. That's why it amazes me how so call Christians so easily give into allowing multiple partners in their lives. Maybe if churches didn't spend so much time criticizing other denominations, we might manage to remember the teachings against fornication. This, *'everyone is going to hell but us'* philosophy sound stupid coming out of any pulpit. I'm not an authority and no one else on earth is either but I can guarantee that constantly putting down another denomination or race is not the way to get into heaven. With all the chaos and constant struggle to survive, most people figure they in hell already. I knew too many floaters, too many worthless men. Reed was supposed to be different. If Star was right, then I was wasting my time.

A Modern Romance

Short Story Collection

A Social Experiment

Would society's issues change if half the world was convinced they discovered the only true daughter of God? This is what happen to Felicitee because of a social experiment spiraling out of control. Felicitee know she is a mortal being who desire to love and be loved. Could Ronan Babtiste be that man? Will her impassioned followers allow it?

She squinted her eyes, contemplating his absurd proposal.

"Do you believe in God?"

"I believe in a supreme being, a higher consciousness."

Good answer, she thought. "Do you in any way believe the hype surrounding me in the past that I am the one and only true daughter of God?"

His long pause spoke volumes. She knew there were those still around who did believe this social experiment she and her roommate had cooked up to prove how susceptible, influential the human mind is to the power of suggestion.

Of course, it wasn't supposed to go as far as it did. Felicitee was forced to go underground for a few years that included a few cosmetic changes before emerging as a clothing designer who garnered wealth beyond reason. She looked up as if silently addressing her heavenly father. I want love, I need to be loved... I think I'm in love with this man. Her faith believed that if it wasn't meant to be, she and Ronan were doomed from the start. We think we're in control, but she strongly felt as he did – that a higher power was directing humanity's path, preparing us for the inconceivable.

"Felicitee."

The sound of his voice brought her out of her overanalytical, swirling thoughts.

Shaleah Hart & Eddie Lancing

Eddie Lancing was her High School boyfriend and love of Shaleah's life. But Eddie had been too unreliable and eventually had to give him the space he needed. Now years later Eddie is back in town for a visit. Will she be able to stop herself from being heartbroken once more? Will Eddie turn out to be the man she always hoped he was?

"Shaleah, a lot has happened since that night at my sister's place. I managed to finally find a career I like. A job offer brought me back to Chicago where I can be closer to my family, but Atlanta feels more like home to me now and ..."

And suddenly she didn't want to hear anymore or why they couldn't be together especially after the last few wonderful days they'd spent together. Eddie Lancing could be a conceited jerk, but he wasn't. Just being around him, his articulate super cool aura and genuine integrity reminded her of the type she prefers but ridiculously hard to find. Quickly gathering up her things. *"You don't have to sour the milk Eddie. I have no illusions about us. It was good to see you again. Hey, it's been fun."*

"Shaleah wait."

Ending it this way, she wouldn't be sitting around waiting for a phone call, text message or email that would never come. See you on Facebook she thought returning to her real world.

Tyre & The Twins

This author vividly shows us the filthy pool of frustrations single people must swim through to finally find happiness. Love is finding your best friend who is not always running hot and cold with their emotions and actions. This short romance will tug at your heart but leave you smiling in the end.

Ernesto snatched Breona's purse out of her hands and slung it across the room. *"You're not going anywhere! You come over here and drink my booze, eat my food, and don't put out!"* He angrily raised his middle finger close to her face.

"You invited me over here," she calmly informed him, not that he was hearing or seeing things in a logical way with all the vodka he'd downed the night before, and he was still drinking shots at 9:00 AM. Earlier she'd pretended to be asleep while he paced the living room crying like a baby, blubbering incoherent words. She knew something was off but now, after their four-year association, he couldn't hide his disdain for women, for the diverse races flowing through his blood, for just about everything on the planet. This guy hated the world and looked for trouble. But his tears were more

about knowing it would be his own self-destructive habits and obnoxious personality that would eventually ruin his life.

"I love you, I love you," he was now saying, too close to her face, then growling like an animal with a maniacal look on his face.

Calling her the b-word next got his face slapped. *"I told you not to call me that!"* They tussled when he pushed her, pinning her down on his lumpy old sofa. *"You can't keep me here,"* she warned seriously, ready to leave his dungeon of a home. For several months she'd tried to end things with this hyper, arrogant loudmouth, a deteriorating attorney who could barely keep clients.

A Modern Romance Suspense

Every Blue Moon

They have an instant attraction, but Avery Louis was too good to be true. If his job is truly noble, Sakira Kelly want in.

Soon after arriving at her Chicago lakefront condo just after daybreak, Sakira threw on her sweats and dashed out for a quick run, her favorite songs in crystal clear stereo soothing her rattled nerves. Spontaneously, she swiped her card pulling out a jiffy bike and like the song blasting in her ear; she rode like the wind, feeling free again. Avery on her mind and a prayer in her heart- not even the traffic annoyed her like she allowed it to do in previous times as she headed for the lakeshore bike path. He was wonderful, mysterious and a missionary.

He was too good to be true and yet she had spoken to him. Surely, she didn't just talk to a ghost. They laughed together and yet she wondered again if what she experienced was real, especially when he didn't come back. She'd gotten so caught up in the seminar it wasn't until it started winding down that she realized he was nowhere to be found.

Work Ethic

Amani dream of owning her own spa resort and Quinn is looking to invest. Together they challenge each other to make this project happen. Their challenges include, inner city drama, sabotage and mysterious new neighbors with a job offer. Their perilous journey cause emotions to run high throwing their relationship in a more romantic direction. Can a good work ethic make their dream come true?

This was the disconnect Amani felt with most of her girlfriends in the neighborhoods. Always talking about sex and chasing down boys was their priority. They dismissed her enthusiasm for owning her own business one day. But Quinn never did. They would sit out on his or her front porch and throw around ideas for hours and grew closer as a result. Quinn had two older brothers. The first one went off to college and later relocated. The second joined the Coast Guard and made a career of it. This inspired them both, and they decided early on they wanted to go to college and experience campus life. They couldn't consider running a business without proper education. It was a starting point anyway. Having worked part time jobs all through their high school years, they couldn't see working for someone else the rest of their life.

<u>In Too Deep</u>

Former co-workers, Javen and Kess meet up on a cruise to settle unfinished business when unexpected events intervene.

"What I said before, it was pure speculation Kess." *More like wishful thinking,* he admitted only to himself. Javen put his fork down sitting back looking right into her eyes. Her intoxicating, bewitching eyes that triggered a driving need so strong it shocked even him. He didn't think himself cable of desiring anyone as much as he did Kess. It made him feel weak and vulnerable and that collided with his tough self-image. For a brief time, the silence between them was deafening as if they'd fallen into a sink hole. He released a deep breath. "I'm willing to acknowledge there's something here but undefined for me at this point." He finally said.

She felt like throwing him overboard without a life-raft for trampling her feelings the way he just did. In the past, fellow team members had described him as running hot and cold never knowing when exactly he may come out of an indifferent bag. But Javen had always been friendly, open and even a bit flirty with her which is why months ago, she felt comfortable reconnecting by suggesting he join her on this week-long cruise. Frankly she was surprised he accepted. But it had been a long time and needed to close this association out as the feeling of unfinished business was too strong to ignore.

NON-FICTION

Inside A Writer's Life

My Grandfather's House

The house is in the heart of an impoverished inner city African American community. Although her Dad inherited the barely affordable distressed property more than twenty years ago, this writer will always think of it as her grandfather's house. It is in this house, this community where she proudly, despite the distractions wrote her last three books. From fending off a former boyfriend turn crack head to dealing with a headstrong yet too sympathetic landlord and his disruptive non-rent paying tenants. This account of a writer's life is about relationships and how they connect to the author's writings. Witness firsthand how a writer struggle to stay motivated and focused in a high-volume environment. *"I'm not looking to sensationalize anything but tell it like it is. Just like there is a duality in most of us, so it is in me. I say let it roll like I'm really feeling it!"* A Behind the Scenes Nine-Year Journey of a Published Author! Looking To Sell As A Screen Adaptation.

The uptown neighborhood I was moving from was a mixture of good and bad with condos right across the street, a huge park area, the beach and the lake just a block away. The community consisted of the well to do, government dependent to the downright poor that included halfway houses and homeless shelters. I could sit in my tenth-floor window and count the sailboats on the lake. In the summer I enjoyed an intoxicating breeze that calmed my spirit reminding me that there were still a few simple pleasures left.

This area offered two recently remodeled major grocery store chains in walking distance. There was a decent strip mall with a hardware store, clothing store and electronics store and didn't see a lot of people hanging out in the parking lot. There were several nice pizza places and even an outdoor café right up the street. Only a block away was a huge McDonalds that stayed busy. On that same side street, you could walk one block east to catch an express bus that jumped on Lake Shore drive with its first stop right in front of water Tower Place on Michigan Avenue.

In the other direction there is a nice size post office and well-kept Laundromat directly across the street. The overall vibe here was pleasant but I was spoiled with the years I'd already spent living closer to downtown in Chicago's Lincoln Park. The basement flat I agreed to move into did offer more space and my desk wouldn't be squeezed in the corner of this one-bedroom apartment where I spent most of my time writing. In this vintage high-rise building I did like how visitors had to sign in downstairs providing the type of upscale vibe I prefer. Occasionally hearing the bedroom neighbor get sucked off by a local whore didn't bother me as much as the endless roaches and mice did.

Then it was the mix race couple on the other side of my living room that found it necessary to loudly beat the hell out of each other every other night. The baby would regularly get cursed out for crying too much. This couple sound as if they enjoyed such routine activity considering the defensive posture they took with the police. Within thirty days after their arrival and just before I moved, the police had busted their door down five times. The manager told me on moving day the minor children had recently been removed by DCFS and the couple couldn't understand why they were being asked to leave.

I knew one of the units on my floor was selling drugs or selling something because of the frequent activity, the constant knocking and occasional fires set off in the rubbish room. But this wasn't considered a bad neighborhood or the hood. That's where I was moving.

Here, I was just a wannabe admiring the unaffordable nice condominiums across the street. Not much different from living on the other side of the railroad tracks in the old south. I could've tried another floor in the building instead of clear across town to yet another questionable neighborhood. But this was a family owned building I would be moving into. A situation I assumed come with perks. Like being able to play my music as loud as I want or hold more than just the threat of eviction over any undesirable tenants. When I first move here, the public library is the only decent thing in walking distance and it could use some updating. I'm always pleasantly surprised at how many people are in there. Even though my Dad had inherited this building over 20 years ago, I knew I would always think of it as my Grandfathers house.

An Author's View On Writing

Have you always wanted to write a book but not sure where to start? Author Sherrie Lynn has packed her personal experiences and condensed information into this fun, easy to follow overview for the novice writer.

In a memoir you're given permission to let your thoughts ponder. How you felt then and looking back on it now. This is expected. Each person or event you choose to profile should be pertinent to the overall theme of your personal story. When proof reading you will eventually see yourself as a character in a fiction story and that will help you be objective and dig deeper.

With fiction your first draft is getting the scenes you really want in the book first. Each time you go over it add more details like the song that was being played over and over on the radio during that time or the top television shows, who's album you just had to buy and why. Also search the Internet for what was playing out in the news. If you keep a journal to start your first draft, you'll have all this information perhaps even too much. Touch on it just enough so the reader is with you on this journey.

An Author's View On Happiness

A thoughtful little non-fiction book that explores the happiness of humanity and the struggle of many to achieve happiness. Lynn shares her views on a range of selected subjects, including: The importance of goal-setting. The truth about time management and how it can increase happiness. The very things that many might view as happiness-inducing are, in fact merely cultivating an insensitivity towards humanity and its core happiness levels! By rediscovering the roots of happiness, humanity can learn how to truly be happy again, through developing a matrix of interpersonal social skills, faith and prioritizing. This is a book you will want to read again and again as a reminder to… Be Happy!

Don't wrap yourself up with all the negativity of the world. In building self-esteem, we must learn how to make the best out of the worst situations. Look at what you're looking at and avoid a negative world view.

Some of us know at least one person who hates everything or never has anything good to say. Too many of us have just developed a habit of seeing the glass half empty as opposed to assuming it's half full. Your first task is to limit the amount of time you spend around folks who appear to be locked in a nowhere zone with no desire to change. This type is not your pet you have to take care of or try and change.

It's not a good idea to put anyone on a high pedestal, including ourselves. To build your own self-image you must observe from a distance other people's behavior. The bulldozers, snobs, gossipmongers, whiners, backstabbers, the walking wounded, controllers, naggers, complainers, exploders, users, and leaches are the type of people who carry bad vibes for your self-esteem, as well as your self-improvement outline. Such types seek you out, so you can't avoid them all, but you will have to learn how to handle them.

Limit your time with poor listeners and people who don't understand most of what you say. They are trying to build their own world and will never respond to you in a way that makes any sense. Pride will keep many of us from admitting what we don't know. Have you noticed how poor listeners expect you to pay attention to whatever they are saying? This type is wasting your time because what they know is limited as they rarely allow new potentially valuable information in.

An Author's View On Humanity

Also known as,

I'll Holler At You! Personal Essays With An Edge

Lively and entertaining best describes this candid, in your face collection of, viciously positive essays on various issues important to the author, and maybe a few other folks out there.

We overtly exploit our sadly digressive intellect and social interactive skills. Discretion and integrity hold little or no meaning anymore. We whine and cry about everything under and over the sun daily and treat our fellow human being like chewed gum stuck to the bottom of our shoe. Yet we're surprised and shocked when one of us falls out of character, becoming a person we don't recognize.

We have witnessed the miracle of having gone from living in caves to skyscrapers; communicating by carving pictures in stone, to smart phones, and now the global wonder of the information super-highway, the world-wide web.

We need to de-emphasize the need for greed and emphasize the necessity of self-development.

Our paranoid, un-accepting intellect is not ready for first contact. We haven't figured out how to protect ourselves from each other. We're so unwittingly contentious; we proudly hold our conflicts for the next generation.

We honor our past ignorance.

Saturating our televised subconscious mind with a unified sense of well-being can start the domino effect we need to clean up the mess we've made.

Phasers on stunned.

This is our foundation:

'Good.'

The platform from which we build and blossom.

Is anyone listening?

Today, most of us are so full of ourselves or disgusted with humanity that we've become immune, deaf to the teachings in our church.

The end of the world?

I truly hope it is the end of this nauseating trip through the lower recesses of our mind. Our mind communities, states and countries rest in a home we call earth. Let's clean it up; let's clean up our home!

Soren & Tanis

A Modern Romance Bonus Short

The setting is designed to be anywhere and the dialog between this couple is spot on addressing society issues. This is sure to be a classic. A rhyming short story.

"Abused from birth, affecting self-worth. Distorted facts create disturbing acts! I know over all it's a mutual understanding we wish to create. A meeting of the minds would set the record straight. But it's also a sad direction in which our expectations turn when discovering one who has yet to learn. Some of us take it for granted but lucky to have a roof over our head, fortunate to have a warm bed. We're blessed to have food to eat, blessed we're not forced to live on the street.   We can provide support to each other when the chips are down and be glad this person is willing to stick around."

"Soren, we're close but so far apart. As a child did this all start. We always avoided questions like, why? When? And fair. A friendship such as ours is indeed rare. But maybe for some greater reason we have never been. I'm convinced I'm destined to drift in a cold indifferent wind.

"Tanis, it's time that create a solid base, to enable us to handle the drama we might face. A warm hug has more to say then kisses with an easy lay. Our need for compassion can leave us weak, natures demand is tough to beat.

"Maybe your right Soren, we need to take time and learn to chill. Hey maybe one day I can cook you your favorite meal. Than we can stroll through the park or by the lake. We need to laugh more for goodness sake. This summer I want to visit that new amusement park where we would have the time of our life. Let's take a break from a world that's not quite right."

ABOUT THE AUTHOR

Sherrie Lynn was born third of four Children and graduated from Chicago's Austin High School. She majored in journalism and commercial art at Wilber Wright College. She worked full time for ten years at a catholic hospital eventually becoming an Illinois state licensed pharmacy technician. In 1992 her first poem titled *The Ivory Key* was published in Over the Rainbow Volume II Poetry Magic Publications. Followed by *Quiet!* in Cherished Poems of The Western World, *Remember Me* in Distinguished Poets of America, and *Momentum* in Whispers II. In 1997 her first short story *Last Stop!* is published in The Storyteller. In 2000 her short story *These People* won a writing competition sponsored by Write Now magazine (Jan/Feb issue) In 1996 the essay, *So Let It Be Written* garnered an honorable mention in Iliad Literary Awards. Lynn has been writing for over thirty-years and should be proud to have produced some of her own designs on marketing flyers, video book trailers and book covers. See full bio at: www.sherrielynn.com